THE MODERN GIRL'S PLAYBOOK

LOOKS LIKE *a Girl* LIVES HERE

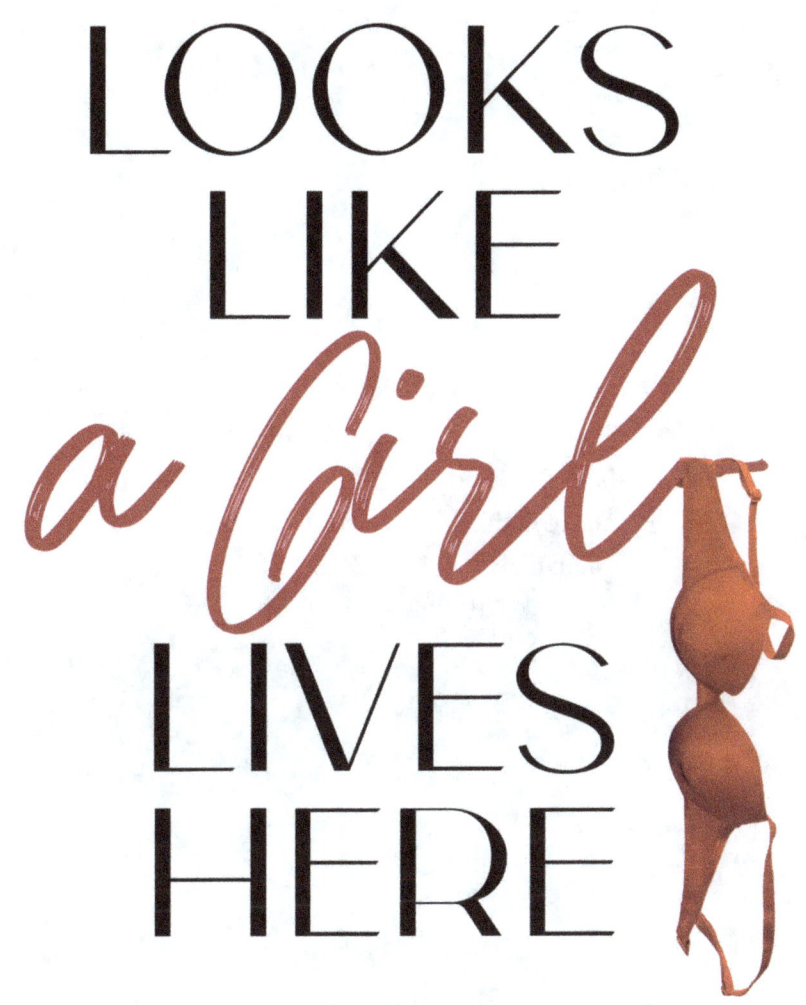

MONICA MARIE

Copyright 2024 by Monica Marie
Published 2024 by ACINOM ZETROC LLC
Printed in the United States of America
ISBN 979-8-9893789-9-9
All rights reserved

Looks Like A Girl Lives Here
The Modern Girl's Playbook
First Edition, Volume I

by Monica Marie

based only
on real events
& real girls

DEDICATION

to my family
to my girlfriends
to my therapist

& to myself

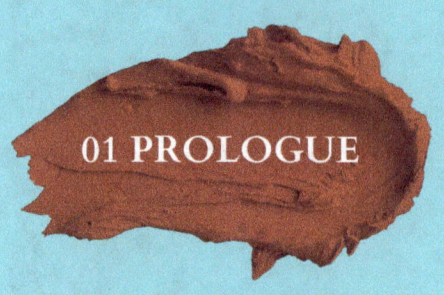
01 PROLOGUE

09 ACT I

47 ACT II

 107 INTERMISSION

 121 ACT III

 133 EPILOGUE

PROLOGUE

GIRL HEART,

I write the majority of these pages at my all time favorite café wearing my favorite high heels decked in my favorite perfume.

I'm wearing the beautiful linen trousers that I found from an *Instagram* ad, stitched with eyelashes and silhouettes of the most desirable high cheek bones & exotic almond eyes.

I'VE TAGGED THE COMPANY
ABOUT 15 TIMES
BUT STILL,
I REMAIN #UNSPONSORED.

FULFILLED

I've paid $3.10 for my café au lait,
always steamed and frothed to perfection.
I write with a hot pink mechanical pencil
as my signature red pen awaits to be called on
for her special debut
that is
daily.

My lips are lined in *Kylie*
& filled with *Charlotte Tilbury*.
Consigned and in gold,
my chain link watch clicks on the counter
every few keystrokes,
& my girlish heart is enamored by the sound.
I'd rather get it scratched,
than let my dainty wrist go bare,
or my outfit,
unfinished.

Black,
oversized sunglasses
& a standby red lipstick
decorate my unofficial workstation,
the one at the big picture window,
flamboyáns in bloom and in view,
at the *5th Avenue Coffee Company & 6th Street Diner*
that I love so much.

Here, I often enjoy the quiche of the day,
made fresh with spinach and savory feta,
from the chefs just behind me.

CHEF,
I hope you see,
in real life,
after red lipstick
& after a fancy coffee,
that I'm shoving this quiche
into my mouth
with my bare hands,
dipping every piece
of perfect flaky crust
into this delicious mango chutney,
walking away pages later,
hours later,
with crumbs still on my face.

I am hungry,
the quiche, divine,
chutney, sweet,
view, exquisite,
& my girl heart,
fulfilled.

ACT I

[SCENE]

SUBJECT: Welcome Home

Hi Monica,
All is ready for you. TVs are on, water is on, & the garage door opener is on the kitchen counter.

See you at 4:15pm to give you your keys.

−Rosemary

Sent from my *iPhone*

ONE MONTH EARLIER

IT WAS THE 15TH OF MARCH
when I laid my head to rest
on an unfamiliar pillow,
finding that the fluff and the feathers
were settled
in all the wrong places
for necks that weren't mine.
The bedsheets didn't graze my skin
the way they used to
just the night before,
& the fan didn't work
in the home that wasn't mine
but I had just gotten the keys to.

"Enjoy & be happy,"
Rosemary said to me
earlier that evening.
For the next six months,
Rosemary would be the landlord
of my new-to-me but slightly old
furnished apartment,
& the words,
be happy,
intrigued me.

Well, Rosemary,
about five minutes ago,
my marriage came to a screeching halt
& my future took a detour
to a destination, unknown.
So how about we start with those keys
& maybe a nap
& I'll unpack my things
& overthink
about what the heck
is even happening.

I'd imagine that when prompted
to be happy,
let alone by a stranger,
I tilted my head
like a dog
when its owner says fun words
like walk
or treat
or park.

But destination unknown,
I can look you in the eye and
I can tell you the truth
that before those keys touched my hand,
I had already made my choice.

I decided
that the least I would do was create,
eventually,
something,
anything,
tangible,
maybe even three dimensional,
something good,
something fabulous,
from this premature midlife crisis
that I quite literally selected
from a hand of circumstances
& said,
this one,
I'll take it,
& I'll figure out the rest as I go.

I didn't know
what this could look like
at the time,
my promise in one hand,
& keys in the other.

Meanwhile, I did just about all the things a girl in my shoes would do in those first thirty days, with the exception of listening to love songs and watching romantic comedies with happy endings.

Instead, I watched the full collection of *Sex & The City* reruns from the '90s, where I lived amongst other lives of other girls, who also, under every set of circumstances, never once compromised on the outfit. I listened to a lot of really girly music, which I curated into a playlist as a forever souvenir of the cards in my hand.

I read a lot of self help books and had some serious talks with The Universe, plotting each and every one of my life's future successes that would stem from this very moment in time. It was as if I was drafting a map from scratch, but with only one road to follow.

If you can hear the sound of my voice right now, spoiler alert.

SOMETHING GOOD.
SOMETHING FABULOUS.

[SCENE]

I press record
as I perform
my evening skin care routine.
Cleanse. Tone. Tighten. Glow.
& moisturize of course.
Under the eye, too.
Ring finger.
Gentle.
Like we were taught to do.

I turn off the water and grab my face towel,
patting down my eyebrows and down to my neck.
In the mirror,
I look at myself from the left,
& then the right.

THURSDAY NIGHT

There at my bedside,
I review the video footage in my camera roll,
pausing halfway through.
"Monica, you're a *writer*. Not a skin care influencer."

I sigh, relocating the video to my phone's virtual trash bin
where it belongs.

Do Not Disturb.
Click.
Y'all can reach me in the morning.

**THE CLOCK ON MY NIGHTSTAND READS 9PM
AS I FOLD MYSELF INTO THE SHEETS.**

And from the other side of my king size bed,
I reach for the stack.
Books on manifestation
& writing motivation,
journals of my writing
& writing utensils
to keep on writing
about all the things I wanted
to write about.

Perhaps if I slept close enough
to all these words,
I'd dream of them
& maybe eventually
wake up to a sentence
or two
of my own.

On this night,
I chose
Marianne Williamson,
author of
A Return to Love.

**THE CLOCK ON MY NIGHTSTAND READS 11PM
AS I GRAB THE PINK HIGHLIGHTER FROM THE STACK.**

"I am willing to see this differently…," from page 38,
now highlighted in pink.

I'm a firm believer that one should stop reading when they've approached words worth remembering. Revel in them a little longer instead of hurrying to read further. These words in pink were mine so I called it a night. I tossed the book to the top of the pile as my red pen slid down the stack and onto the top sheet. Lights out.

My eyes settle into the darkness, and I, into my evening ritual.

**"OKAY, UNIVERSE.
I AM WILLING TO VIEW
MY PREMATURE MIDLIFE CRISIS
DIFFERENTLY.
I DON'T REALLY KNOW
HOW THAT WORKS
BUT LET'S JUST SAY MY
SUGGESTION BOX IS OPEN.
AMEN, NAMASTE,
GRATITUDE ALWAYS,
& GOOD NIGHT."**

[SCENE]

The birds outside my window wake me,
followed by the tick tock of the clock.

With my eyes still closed,
& head rested on the pillow,
I begin sifting through my closet.

*How about we keep it simple today,
with our go-to trousers
which will go with just about any dramatic top,
OH!
Like the bandage neon green one
or the hot pink feather halter.
Both would match our go-to pair of heels
that we know we're gonna wear.
Not to mention,
they're beaded with both neon green and hot pink.
How convenient, I think.*

My heart begins to race with excitement
as I toss to my other side.

FRIDAY MORNING

how many days since I last washed my hair?

Three?
Or is it four?
Did my hair tie leave a kink after my workout last night?
More important, how bad does it smell?

With my eyes still closed,
& head rested on the pillow,
I grab my hair
& pull it under my nose.

Eh, tolerable.

I toss back to the other side,
awake enough now to open my eyes
& look at the time.

I mean, it's only 7:30am.
Technically I have time to curl my hair.
& if I do curl my hair,
what earrings would I wear?
Wait, I have the perfect pair!
Alright, let's do this!
Now, we're not gonna scroll on our phone
until after we make our bed
because we're creating boundaries, remember?

{ **IF YOU MAKE YOUR BED IN THE MORNING, YOU HAVE A BAZILLION TIMES HIGHER CHANCE OF BECOMING A BAZILLIONAIRE...** }

I always mock the videos that circulate social media
about the supposed direct correlation
between how much money you will make
if and only if you make your bed in the morning.

Yet, here I am,
proudly,
making my bed for the sixth month in a row,
with last year's *TikTok*-inspired New Year's Resolution to blame.

Okay, now you can touch the phone.

I bring my thumb and index finger together in each hand
for a moment to relish at how awesome I'm becoming.

"ALEXA! PLAY MY PREMATURE MIDLIFE CRISIS PLAYLIST ON SPOTIFY."

Before I know it,
I am put back together again
in the outfit from my imagination.
I bathe myself in perfume
& am ready to choose the day's shade
from my lipstick drawer,
never to be chosen
without extreme consideration.

**BECAUSE, GIRLS!
Never underestimate
the power of
getting dolled up,
dressed up,
& showing out
for none other
than yourself.**

[SCENE]

Sunset on the patio with a mocktail,
seltzer water,
lime flavor,
mint leaves,
& a lemon squeeze.

I have, for myself,
half a French baguette about to go bad
& no, I'm not gonna make croutons out of it.
On a plate,
some leftover salami slices and a block of gouda cheese,
garnished with a sprig of cotton candy grapes for color.

CHARCUTERIE FOR DINNER
& A GIRL COULDN'T BE HAPPIER.

Feet up. Fuzzy socks on. Blanket, check.
& the perfect night in.

FRIDAY NIGHT

Upcoming Period 1h ago
Your period will likely start in the next 7 days.

[SCENE]

Saturday morning
& I wake again to my stack
helping to keep the other side of the bed warm.
& my signature red pen who finally had her
way with the top sheet last night.

I stretch
& yawn
& walk out of my room
& open the balcony door
for another Saturday sunrise with myself
when
the
sun
hit
different.

SATURDAY MORNING

First, the outdoor vase of flowers catch my eye. The happiest of yellow sunflowers amongst fragrant eucalyptus & barely white baby's breath. Then, the blanket still falling from the brown wicker couch, as if I had just gotten up. My gold hoop earrings thrown onto the coffee table, subtle yet dramatic, glimmering in the morning sun. And a lip balm gone rogue, cradled by the crease of two couch cushions. I can feel these diamonds of delight fill my eyes when I say the following words aloud, with undertones of mischief, wonder, and excitement...

> **...IT LOOKS LIKE A GIRL LIVES HERE.**

Next to the living room lamp was last night's hair clip & over there in the corner, a basket of girl shoes, and in whichever direction my eyes moved, hair ties with the hair still stuck to them. All of my emotional-shopping shopping bags and my lacey red bra thrown over the wing back chair. My *Kate Spade* bathmats and *Bath & Body Works* candles and all the throw pillows I never needed. Everything, the gender role of pink, on purpose. High heel shoes and *New Yorker* magazines, and each of my lipsticks resting comfortably in every shade on every surface. And then the makeup infused face towels and revenge body leggings overflowing from my hamper onto the closet floor. My blue light lenses were still left on the couch and left on the counter, the glass from last night's mocktail, stemless, and embellished in rhinestones. So many rhinestones that I'll need to wash it by hand. But because of the girliness of it all, I'm happy to. Because then in the distance, I saw the heating pad still plugged into the wall that luckily was turned off ---

**MY
APARTMENT
WAS
CANDY COATED
IN GIRL.**

I STARTED
INTENTIONALLY LEAVING MY BRAS
IN LACE,
IN PUSH UP AND IN DEMI,
MESH AND BANDEAU,
& IN SULTRY BLACK AND BROWN
CHEETAH PRINT,
MY FAVORITE
BUT HARDLY WORN,
WHEREVER THEY WANTED TO LAND.

I STARTED
LEAVING MY PANTS ON THE FLOOR
WITH THE LEGS STILL IN THEM
AND WALKING
STRAIGHT OUT OF THE ROOM
WITH MY SHOULDERS
IN THEIR BACK POCKETS.
NOT BECAUSE I WAS IN A RUSH,
BUT BECAUSE I WAS HOOKED
ON WATCHING MY GIRL MESS
LIVE A LIFE OF HER OWN.

I discovered a new love
for that cold second sink,
barren,
unused,
& really
underutilized.
Because there,
I could store my curling iron
& my hair dryer,
which I hoped could work some magic
in encouraging me everyday
to either wash my hair
or make what's often six-day-old-hair
look a little better.

As days went by
& each of the two cords
dangled down from the countertop,
I began to grin at the tripping hazard.
It was the perfect outfit
of girl and mess
that I grew to look forward to.

I itch my scalp as I write this, digging my freshly manicured nails through my slicked back bun of glorified, glamorized, six-day-old-hair, secured with a red velvet scrunchie, and the look, complete, by a pair of my most detailed earrings to distract from the truth my hair didn't wish to tell.

I'll wash my hair tomorrow,
SAYS EVERY GIRL EVER.

Me being one of them, as I posted a video of
today-is-not-the-day-for-hair-wash-day
to my feed.

> "You're making my scalp itch!
> But wait, is that chrome I see on your nails?
>
> YES!
>
> Why didn't you tell me?!
> I got chrome, too!
>
> No way! #TWINNING!"

the GIRL WAS GIRLING

FROM THE BIG PICTURE WINDOW AT MY FAVORITE CAFE

from my left

two young girls walk by, both in single shoulder
crop crops, torn jean shorts, and sneakers,
& I knew very well the thread of
what are you wearing text messages
that were exchanged that same morning.

from my right

a mother takes a photo for her daughter,
posing on an assumed vacation.
After the phone captures the photo,
she grabbed it out of her mother's hands
& immediately opened her social media to post it.

BEFORE MY EYES, WITH JUST A LITTLE BIT OF TIME, my sights were turned away from the unexciting break up reel that had been playing, over and over, like a broken *Instagram* algorithm. My attention, now diverted to this unexpected unraveling of everyday girl things, one by one, like scenes of a play, starring girls who were just like me, saying the things I say, & doing the things I know I do, too.

& so, just like me, after my order with *DoorDash* has been placed, the candle has been lit, and I've nestled into the couch under a blanket, savoring a moment in time where I have nowhere to be but scrolling through memes and sharing them all with my girlfriends, I imagined that to be how this could play out for other girls, too. Maybe a girl like you. One #relatable scenario after another, having nearly nothing to do with the one that came before, yet because the algorithm *does* work, they have everything to do with each other. Just short enough to match our modern day attention spans and just accurate enough to make us say...

"oh my gosh this is totally us!"

ACT II

GET READY WITH ME FOR A DAY IN THE LIFE OF A GIRL

LIVING IN THE MODERN WORLD

LIKE,
when I took notice of the natural arrangement of girlhood
that created herself on my dresser,

outfitted in earrings in various shapes and sizes,
bedazzled by rings and bangles for daily occasions,
grab and go lip gloss and *Classic Cherry Chapstick*.

All of which were showcased against a backdrop of perfume,
an assortment made of complimentary samples,
not good enough to be purchased with real money,
but good enough to be worn for free.

& just as another sun sets,
& after a bra decided not to be worn,
I'll rip off my pasties
throwing them right into the mix.
Amongst the lipstick,
amongst the perfume.
Delighted by the sound of earring backs
landing amongst the others.

The most picturesque display of
the girl that lives here.

Time and again,
me and my long distance gal pal
will embark on our favorite
Snapchat game.

**I'LL SHOW YOU MY ROOM
IF YOU SHOW ME YOURS,**

& compare
whose is more of a disaster.

Whose vertical collections
of wear again,
not dirty enough,
categorized
& organized
piles of clothes
& emergency laundry
& dry clean only
are taller,
wider,
more...navigable?

**"HOW MUCH OF THAT PILE
IS ACTUALLY CLEAN?"**

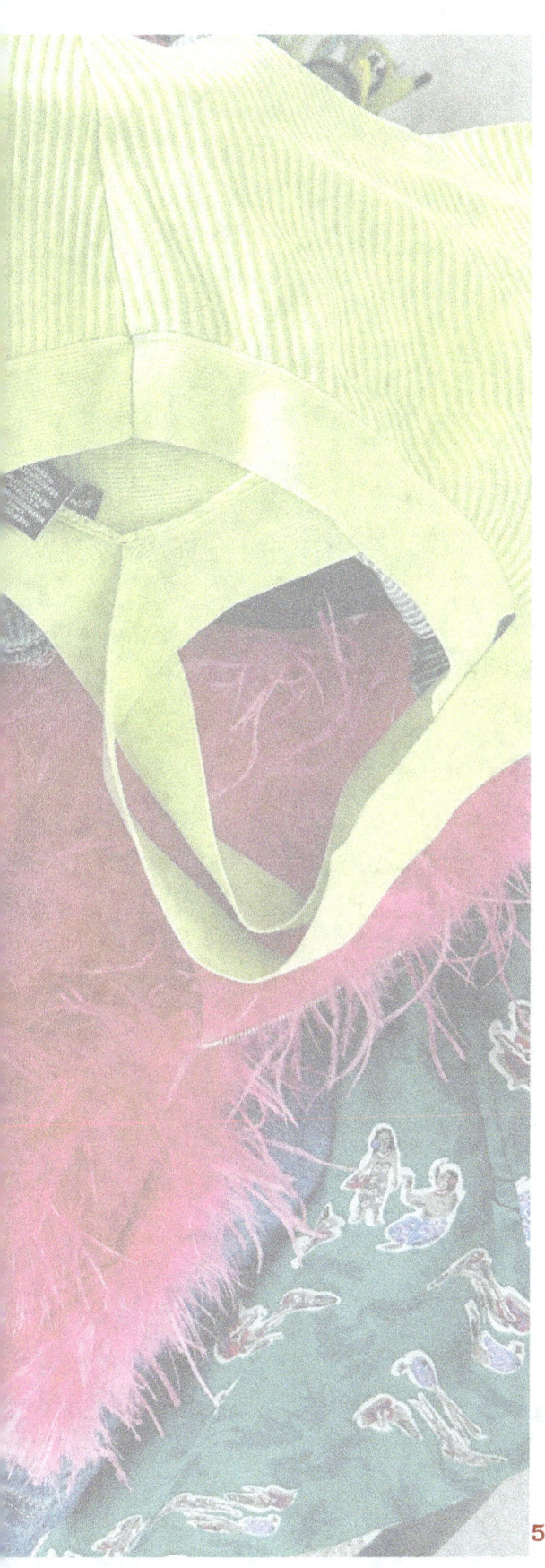

"SO, I'M PROBABLY NEVER GONNA WEAR THESE, YOU WANT 'EM?"

The pile that's always topped
with the forgotten pair of shoes
that oh so desperately tried
to be worn last week.
The ones who thought it was their time to shine
after two years of living in their box
with the stuffing still inside the soles,
only to be outvoted
by the die hard nude ones instead,
the ones whose heels have been super glued
once maybe twice
& with blood embedded in the straps.

I'd like to call this
GIRL PSYCHOLOGY,
reserved for me,
the girlfriends I call mine,
& the ones you call yours.

#GRWM

AN ODE TO THE #GRWM GIRLS AND THE #OOTD GIRLS, BECAUSE HIDING IN A CORNER SOMEWHERE IN THAT GIRLY ROOM OF YOURS, I ASSUME THERE TO BE A HEAPING PILE OF CLOTHES THAT YOU, TOO, HAVE TO DEAL WITH AS A RESULT OF SELECTING THE OUTFIT AND PERFECTING THE SHOT.
& BECAUSE OF THE #CLEANMYAPARTMENTWITHME GIRLS, YOU MIGHT FEEL LIKE YOU NEED TO IMMEDIATELY CLEAN UP AFTER YOURSELVES, BECAUSE IT WILL SET THE TONE FOR YOUR DAY OR MAKE YOU FEEL MORE PRODUCTIVE LIKE THE #PRODUCTIVITYHACK GIRLS TOLD YOU IN A POST LAST WEEK, THE ONE THAT YOU SCREENSHOTTED ONTO YOUR PHONE NEVER TO BE LOOKED AT AGAIN.

#TRENDING

#FOLLOW

HECK, WHAT DO I KNOW! MAYBE ROCKING YOUR OUTFIT OF THE DAY & POSTING THE SHOT AND CLEANING UP AFTERWARDS REALLY DOES MAKE YOU FEEL LIKE YOU'RE BETTER THAN EVERYONE ELSE & THAT'S BECAUSE YOU ARE. SO, ME AND MY LONG DISTANCE GAL PAL WOULD LIKE TO CORDIALLY INVITE YOU TO THROW YOUR BRA ON THE FLOOR RIGHT NOW. RIP IT OFF. CHUCK IT ON THE GROUND. AND WALK AWAY. YOU'LL FEEL BETTER. OR HAVE A PANIC ATTACK. OR YOUR SIGNIFICANT OTHER WILL COME PICK IT UP AND SIGH LOUD ENOUGH TO MAKE SURE YOU HEAR THEM. #WORTHIT.

[SCENE]

Oh, sorry, I can't today.
YEAH, BECAUSE SHE HAS A NAIL APPOINTMENT.

Standing or not, it's a big day and we can't overcrowd a day like today with too many tasks at once. Say, we're ready for some self care. And by no means can it wait until Sunday because the nail salons are usually closed and we've been inconvenienced by life one too many times this week.

It's Tuesday.
We deserve it.

After all, we still have to rehearse all the way there. Color, shape, gel, dip? Or should we give our nails a break and go natural? Deluxe pedicure with hot stones and a hot towel for twice the cost? Or just the plain standard so we can admire Susan to our left, snoring at her hot stone and towel treatment that we'll know we should have paid extra for?

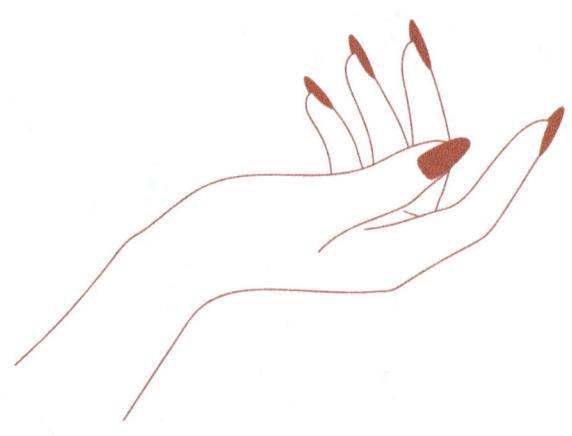

GIRL GOES TO NAIL SALON

I am going to the gyno after this so maybe I do deserve that paraffin wax add-on and ya know what? When my amazing nail tech comes back around, the answer is a resounding YES, I will take a soda even though I don't drink soda because maybe today really is my day.

Meanwhile, we don't know what to do and we don't know where to look when it's time for the foot massage. Close our eyes, maybe? While our bodies get thrown by the wakes of the chair massage, by the knead that hits in all the wrong places, yet feels so right?

Thank you so much because that really was phenomenal is all that really needs to be said.

GIRL,
the sass,
walking out of that nail salon,
on that inconvenienced
self-care-girl-appointments-only-Tuesday.

Am I right?
Unmatched.

Topcoat shining,
cuticles tamed,
& at every red light,
another glance
to admire the color once more.

A MOMENT OF GRATITUDE
TO THE NAIL TECHNICIANS OF OUR LIVES.
FOR KEEPING US STELLAR,
DECKED TO THE NINES,
& FEMININELY FABULOUS.

with love,
THE GIRLS

ICED COFFEE, SUNGLASSES, CREDIT CARD.

All hail my girls of the modern world, where should we go next?

Hobby Lobby
Bath & Body Works
HomeGoods
Target
TJMaxx
Marshalls
Sephora
Ulta
Victoria's Secret
Trader Joe's
Costco

All of the above and in our *Instagram* story,

#ERRANDS

[SCENE]

Off to bask in that badge of honor,
the one we all give ourselves,
the one we paint
on the back
on the front
on the arm
of our non-dominant hand,
painted in moods and possibilities,
envisioned outfits and date nights,
equal strokes bravery and comfort zone,
ol' faithfuls and new me's.
Line after line,
of lipstick color,
eye liner,
eyebrow filler,
lip liner,
eye shimmer,
& just the right shades
of bronzer, blush, and highlighter.

GIRL GOES TO COSMETIC STORE

I DON'T KNOW ABOUT YOU
BUT I'M A SUCKER FOR A NAME,
LIKE,
TOO HOT TO TROT,
THE DEVIL WEARS RED,
OR
SHE'S JUST A BADASS,
CHOOSE THIS ONE.
YES,
AS A MATTER OF FACT,
I'LL BUY IT.

The way we'll walk out of that makeup store
waving our badge of honor with pride.
Because not only can we never find the sanitation station,
but there aren't any puffy things stocked
on that particular day, anyway,
when we have thirty colors,
shades,
& specks of eye shadow
on our hand ---

" --- Ma'am, can I help you find something?"

"No, really, it's fine,"
because it's much more fun to wear our girlhood,
like a stolen accessory,
right out of the store instead.

GIRLS!

what color is the inside of your makeup bag?

NO.
Not the color in which you bought it
brand new from the store.
The color that it is **now**.

Our makeup bags
that wear the makeup themselves,
each their own shade
of porcelain and tan,
bronze and blush,
caramel, mocha,
& deep espresso.
Graffiti of eyeliner
that's been floating around
drying out
with its lid
nowhere to be found.

& no,
the bag need not be replaced.
That would be such a waste of money.
& washing it?
A waste of time.

GIRLS!

what am I?

We have one in the bathroom.
& one in the car.
One on our nightstand,
in the spare bathroom,
& three in every purse.

Some with color,
some without,
some medicated when we need it to work,
some so organic that they don't work.

Found one in the dryer,
which we now must figure out,
which and where needs replaced.
Or maybe let's try to salvage it.

We get them every Christmas,
lose them all by New Year's,
& drive twenty minutes to the store
to get a new one.
Partially because we think we need to,
mainly because it's fun.

THE ANSWER IS ABSOLUTELY ANY FORM OF LIP CARE.

[SCENE]

65% off, everything in the bins.
All the fun bras we kinda wanna buy
but more than likely won't.

Extra straps. Extra padding.
Extra beading. Extra everything.

We sift through each bin,
the one in our size
& the one next to it.

BECAUSE WE ARE THE EVERY GIRL.

Like the one who was here before us,
who grabbed an extravagant bra
& changed her mind
by the time she got to the next bin
where she chose to leave it behind.

GIRL GOES TO LINGERIE STORE

BUT LIKE,
what if we did buy one of the extravagant bras,
just this once,
one that we just might wear
but more than likely won't?

WHAT IF JUST FOR A NIGHT?
SPECIAL SITUATIONSHIPS ONLY?

Maybe that floral balconette bra,
with lace on the cups
& diamonds on the straps
& a zipper in the front.

It wouldn't be see-through
under that one dress we never wear...

...but what if we did?

After a number of daydreams, our right arm is holding three new spicy sale bras like a hanger, very well knowing that we'll never wear any of them. Very well knowing that we need a new black bra, a replacement nude bra, because ours is falling apart and we've worn it past the three stages of **get a new bra** in the back. But, being a girl is the very reason why the lingerie store sells those hot pink bras, cheetah print bras, and those with beads, pearls, and one too many straps. Any good corporate lingerie folk knows...

IF WE'RE ROCKIN'
A FRESH ACRYLIC SET
& A BRAND NEW LIP COLOR
WE'RE NOT GOING HOME
WITHOUT THE
EXTRAVAGANT BRA
EITHER.

[SCENE]

First,
she spends
an undisclosed
amount of time
getting beautified
to perfection.

Purse to match the heel,
lips to match the vibe,
consulting with a girlfriend
to make sure the outfit
is just right.

> **HOW MUCH CLEAVAGE IS TOO MUCH CLEAVAGE?**
>
> **DOES IT LOOK LIKE I'M TRYING TOO HARD?**
>
> **ARE MY HEELS TOO TALL?**

IT'S DATE NIGHT

SHE'S ON HER WAY
just as much as she's on her hands and knees
in a desperate search and rescue
for the transparent earring back that she just dropped.
One might say to use the back from a different pair
but any girl knows that doesn't always work.

SHE'S FASHIONABLY LATE
just as much as she is fresh out of excuses
because at this point in her life,
she is borderline unbelievable.

SHE REALLY IS ON HER WAY NOW,
but first, she admires herself in the mirror.
First from the left and then the right,
like two opportunities to adore herself
because once is never enough.

She struts to the car, tossing her heels to the floor.
Comfort for the drive, grand entrance later.

Can we get a booth please?
SAYS EVERY GIRL EVER.

The thrill of a girl
dressed up,
out,
seen,
& admired.
Her lashes are lashing.
& the highlight on her cheeks is cheeking.

SHE FEELS GOOD.
SHE FEELS FABULOUS.

DATES,
dare not tell her
she's beautiful,
stunning,
absolutely glowing
& like, totally irreplaceable.

& IF THE FOOD DOESN'T MAKE HER DANCE IN HER CHAIR, YOU CHOSE THE WRONG RESTAURANT.

[SCENE]

NO MAN EATS THE WAY A GIRL SNACKS!

In that dance-able restaurant,
or on the couch in our pajamas,
standing inside of the pantry,
or nearly inside of the refrigerator.

We demolish.
We smash.
We are animals.
For those few moments of peace.
Unfiltered. Unhinged. Ravenously unleashed.
& more than likely dipping one thing
into something else.

GIRLS WHO SNACK

If we're eating a snack,
I must warn you that it will be abrupt
when we stop responding to your texts.

HOW CAN WE TEXT YOU BACK IF WE HAVE FOOD IN ONE HAND WHILE THE OTHER IS PULLING CHIP CRUMBS FROM OUR BRA?

If only you could see how happy we are.
Eyes rolling to the back of our head.
The sounds we make.
The mess on our face.

WHAT'S A SERVING SIZE ANYWAY?

FUNYUNS® BRAND ONION FLAVORED RINGS ARE FUN!

FUNYUNS® brand Onion Flavored Rings.

Next time you're in a mood for a snack that's different, try FUNYUNS® brand Onion Flavored Rings. They are a taste sensation that runs rings around other snacks.

Also try them with your favorite dip for a taste sensation that runs rings around other snacks. They are great for picnics, parties and lunches.

Anywhere and enjoy with your family can eat FUNYUNS® brand Onion Flavored Rings are a fun snack...

...TASTE WITH YOUR FAVORITE FOODS.

FUNYUNS® BRAND ONION FLAVORED RINGS!...

**GIRLS,
can you name a better feeling
than eating snacks in your car?
in a parking lot?
straight out of the drive thru?
right out of the grocery bag?**

The car of a girl is witness to a girl who funnels food into her face like you have never seen before. It is the most optimal café. Its own caliber of restaurant, menu options unlimited. Temperature in her control. Pants buttoned or zipped, always optional. A self care escape and daytime nightclub where judgements are off limits and filters don't exist. Because in a girl's car, she can talk out loud to no one, how she feels about that customer who barked at her earlier and the person who looked at her for two seconds too long right after that. She can kiss goodbye her high pitched customer service voice and practice all the juicy comebacks she wished she would have said.

**Taylor Swift.
The occasional heavy metal.
Snacks.**

THERE IS NO BAD DAY THAT CANNOT BE FIXED WITH A GIRL DINNER & CANCELLED PLANS.

...who started this thing called girl dinner anyway?

One night, I bought myself a veggie tray. Family size for family gatherings, just for me. With a handful of fancy breadsticks, an assortment of gourmet cheese, and the night capped with chocolate chips straight out of the *Ghirardelli* bag meant for baking. Not happening.

As I sat my braless self down on the couch, I sighed in #gratitude as *Netflix* chimed me in to a good night.

"~~Sorry, not gonna ——~~"
WHO SAYS I HAVE TO APOLOGIZE?

I trimmed the wick to the night's candle of choice
& pressed send on my [unapologetic] response.

Evening out, cancelled.
Evening in is on.
& the sound of streaming whatever the heck I want.

GIRL!

MAY YOU BE OVERCOME WITH ZEN
& IN LOVE WITH YOUR CONFIDENCE
THAT YOU KNOW YOU OWE
EXPLANATION TO NO ONE
FOR WHY YOU DON'T WANT TO DO
ANYTHING [EVER]
OTHER THAN STAY HOME WITH
YOUR ANIMAL[S].

"
FINE.
Wanna go shopping with me
tomorrow instead?

　　　　　　　　　I really shouldn't be spendi -----

---Oh! I just checked
& I have enough Starbucks rewards
to get us both a free coffee.

　　　　　　　　　Sold. Pick me up at 10.
　　　　　　　　　What are you gonna wear?

　　　　　　　　　　　　Comfy cute?
　　　　　　　　　　　Heels or flats?
　　　　　　　　Or should we go all out?
"

THE FEELING OF A SHOPPING BAG IN A GIRL'S HANDS
[MORE THAN ONE PREFERRED]

The ones from our favorite splurge counters,
our new treasures wrapped and packed
in the smallest shopping bags known to man,
the ones that demonstrate to the world
just how much we can't afford.

Like the plastic bags we get from not spending enough,
the ones with cut out handles that hurt our fingers,
instead of the paper ones
with flat bottoms
& thin woven handles
that fit in our hands so elegantly,
the way a girl's shopping bag should.

Like our new thrifted going out clutch
for all of our [cancelled] going out plans
& brand new base model cars
just for the new car smell.

Like my Mom's incessantly matching pajama sets,
& her adorable koala sleep mask,
equipped with ears and all.
Her bejeweled hair clips
& soft pink aloe vera #SelfCareSunday socks
from the local drug store.

I GOT IT BECAUSE IT WAS PRETTY.
I GOT IT BECAUSE I WANTED IT.

**two things
that girls should practice
saying to whoever is
ridiculous enough to ask**

SELF CARE SUNDAY

Clean. Tidy. Dishes. Laundry.
Fresh flowers and maybe a face mask.

We'll get the healthiest batch of groceries
that we've ever shopped in our lives,
freezer stocked with *Ben & Jerry's*
that won't make it to Monday
because on Monday we'll start all of our
starting–Monday habits.

New week, new me.
I swear, this time.

I really need to start meal prepping,
SAYS EVERY GIRL EVER.

#HOTGIRLWALKING

Beats dropping.
Sun beaming.
Hashtag healing.
& the walk becomes a catwalk.

The sidewalk, carpeted red, a London fashion runway, to strut her sweat and hidden tears and her taste in music that she insists is better than everyone else's and *they just don't get it.*

She'll smile and smirk, looking up at the sky like she's the main character in every movie there ever was. Each lyric sent to her at the perfect moment in space and time, so much and so fitting that she'll insist it was The Universe, nothing less than a sign, to justify that thing she wants to do but desperately knows she shouldn't.

Because later that night, she'll cry in surrender. Maybe manifest a little more and maybe a little too hard, awake with swollen eyes the next morning. She'll cover, conceal, and contour and pull from the makeup bag of excuses for the bags under her eyes in preparation for **GIRLS NIGHT.**

Didn't sleep enough.
Slept too much.
Dehydrated.
Overly hydrated.
Had too much salt.
Had too much sugar.
Scrolled too much last night.
Worked too hard last night.
Stayed up too late last night.
Bad contacts.
Need new glasses.
Need new mascara.
Allergic to the mascara.
Allergic to the pillow case.
Allergic to the laundry detergent.
Watched a really good rom-com
with a really good ending.
Watched a really good rom-com
with a terrible ending.
The weather.

& when in doubt,
blame it on the pollen.

GIRLFRIEND,
LET'S GET REAL
JUST FOR A SEC

Nothing will match the initial high of unboxing that new pair of shoes just like the last dipped chip is never as satisfying as the first. Because eventually the joys of emotional shopping will wear off and the new car smell, not as strong. On Wednesday morning, your mascara will miss the tube and smear all over Tuesday's new nails. Your hair will lay flat, your smile will look weird without reason, your stomach will feel suddenly 10x bigger than ever before, and all of your clothes will suck. So you'll go for white on white, no energy for creativity, and throw your six-day-old-hair into a claw. You won't feel funny anymore and you'll want to take a nap and cancel girls night out but you cancelled last time so you have to go this time. Your 2pm coffee will turn to anxiety and make you question everything that has ever made you happy and you'll think for the longest moment that the joy is gone forever, that it was just here for a short stay. Your career choice will suddenly come into question, filling you with doubt and agony that will suddenly replace what you once called *ugh, I'm so fulfilled* ...just last week.

You'll want to move to the city and open up your own business & become your own girl boss just as much as you want to start a farm and milk cows and live off the land but not as much as you want to splurge on a euro trip because you only live once. And no sooner than you start looking at *Google Flights*, you'll start a spreadsheet for budgeting, effective immediately. On your way to meet the girls, you'll get irritated in the car because your claw clip is rubbing against the head rest so you'll rip it out and press the pedal to the metal, looking like a hot mess on the loose because you can't handle the stress. You'll insist that there's a hair stuck to the back of your elbow but after several failed attempts, you won't be able to find it. Suddenly you'll feel a sneeze coming on, afraid to close your eyes because what if you crash and die? A death grip on the steering wheel, hands becoming clammy.

Hot flash.
Lightheaded.
Should I pull over?
Why am I sweating?
Am I gonna pass out?
Why do I feel like this?

& just my luck,
I'm wearing white.

GIRL, CAN YOU CHECK ME?

WAIT, ARE WE OFFICIALLY CYCLE SYNCED?!

SO THAT'S WHY I WAS CRYING!

YOU'RE GOOD, GIRL.

SERIOUSLY, DOES ANYONE HAVE A TAMPON? I SWITCHED PURSES!

THESE ARE THE THINGS THAT ONLY GIRLS UNDERSTAND.

girls

The way our jewels and purses will rattle and jingle as each of our signature scents fill the room. We flip our hair from side to side just like last month's hairdresser told us not to. The collection of nail colors, hair styles, patterns on our clothing and designs on our shoes will have us complimenting each other like a broken record. We are **hashtag obsessed** with each other.

CATCH UP. INTERROGATE. GOOD GIRL CONFIDENTIALITY MEETS THE HOTTEST OF GOSSIP. UNTIL EVERY LAST DETAIL HAS BEEN OVERTURNED.

We unravel our past like a present and dissect the future like professional fortune tellers and with every piece of unsolicited advice received, we question the need for therapy and how much inner child work we obviously haven't done.

& NO, WE WILL NOT TAKE OUR OWN ADVICE.

night

We will talk about all the things we want and need and holler and rally over how much we all believe in anything and everything any of us have to say. We snap, clap, laugh, and dance over every accomplishment that has yet to even manifest. And everything good, everything fabulous that we're doing while we wait.

that's the thing about girls.

How much we want out of the world for ourselves
but how much more we want to see the girl across from us get it first.
We want to watch our girlfriend do what she said she would do,
achieve what she said she would achieve,
win greater than she ever thought she would win,
and live the life we always knew she deserved.

> "YOU KNOW, WHEN MY GIRLFRIEND IS WINNING, IT'S LOW KEY <u>ME</u> THAT'S WINNING.

WE BOTH WIN BECAUSE OUR MANSIONS ARE ON THE SAME STREET AND WE'RE GONNA NEED EACH OTHER TO HOUSE SIT WHILE THE OTHER IS OUT OF TOWN ON VACATION DURING HER WELL DESERVED EARLY RETIREMENT.

I DON'T THINK THE PEOPLE HEARD YOU. CAN YOU SAY THIS LOUDER?
—"

INTERMISSION

CALLING ALL GIRLS OF TODAY'S MODERN WORLD!
it's your turn.

#RELATABLE
#GIRLTHINGS

WRITING UTENSILS CAN BE BUT ARE NOT LIMITED TO
LIPSTICK, LIP LINER, NAIL POLISH, EYE LINER,
ONE OF YOUR CHILD'S CRAYONS OR COLORED PENCILS,
...WHATEVER YOUR GIRL HEART WANTS.

ACT III

[SCENE]

If this was the beginning of a movie scene with only a few minutes left before the credits roll, after the action, after the drama, and after the laughs I hope you laughed, I'd imagine it to be quiet. A slow Saturday morning. The camera rolling over my king size bed, my freshly washed one-day-old-hair draped weightlessly across my face. The birds chirping outside my window, as they always do. And me, coming out of a comatose sleep, as if a large wave of time has passed.

                                                               & a copy of *The Playbook*
                                         keeping the other side of the bed warm.

FOUR MONTHS LATER

Over the span of these four months, I have taken notice of so many more girl things in this modern world that only girls understand. Like all the flowers I buy for myself and watch die a week later and like the shame I feel now that my nails are grown out and I'm two weeks past due for an appointment and you can totally tell.

However, the greatest glimmers of girl while writing this book came directly from the girls of my life themselves. The ongoing messages, phone calls, and girl conversations that inspired these very pages.

So, as the collection of pages to your right grows slim, I would like to conclude with a collection of girl mementos that played out during the making of *The Playbook*. Because, girls, I want you to know that with every girl-encrypted message, you brought this book to life that much more.

GIRL

One day, I sent a photo to my girlfriend of me using my panty strap as a sweat towel holder on one of my evening runs. She responded by telling me that she used to do the same thing in college to hold her phone on a night out.

Sharing hair and nail photos and hacks for manicuring the fuzz above our upper lip, the fuzz that we don't ever tell the world we have, [until now because I kind of just ratted us out but only with the best of intentions].

Talking about how all we want to do is stay home with our pets and exchange memes of other pets and photos of our own living their best lives. Exchanging lists of what girly movies to watch and for what moods and on what platforms.

Talking about our favorite brands of pasties and which organic deodorants don't suck but also won't give us breast cancer. And one of my favorites was a message from a girlfriend saying that all she wanted for her birthday was a girls night out with girls she actually likes because I know that every girl reading this knows exactly what she means.

Simultaneously, another girlfriend sends me pictures of her beautifully plated girl dinner and the healthy snacks she's stirring up because goals, because protein.

THINGS

A big hug to the girls who sent me messages about the things you were going through in your own lives while I was going through mine during the making of this book.

Exchanging lipstick moments and hard moments and how we feel like new women after hair wash day and a day at the salon. And the girlfriend of mine who went to get a scalp massage as a means of self care and the round of applause that I hope she heard from my end of the thread.

To the girl who said my shoes were feminine and me realizing what a great compliment that was. In that moment, I remember grabbing her hands to tell her how much I loved her nail color and how glad I was that she splurged on the pedicure.

To the girl who wants to talk about new brands and new stores to discover and best products for our hair for when we don't want to wash our hair and going to get blowouts for reasons none other than to feel good and fabulous.

& how at girls night, we'll question which glass belongs to which girl by comparing the lip prints and lip colors, matching the girl to the glass. Borrowing comfy clothes and hair ties and *Chapstick* and blankets to get ready for the perfect movie night with endless snacks that we're not even hungry for.

At last, to the girl who has a conference call with her best girlfriends of 30+ years, where the password to be accepted into the room is literally, girltalk.

DESTINATION,

WITH AN OPEN PERSPECTIVE ON WHATEVER HAND OF CIRCUMSTANCES OR UNINVITED RUDELY TIMED LIFE CRISIS IS IN FRONT OF YOU, YOU CAN ACHIEVE A DIFFERENT OUTCOME. IT MIGHT BE UNEXPECTED. BUT IT MIGHT ALSO BE FABULOUS.

UNKNOWN

...just don't forget to live while you wait. sometimes the fabulous takes place in the waiting.

Today, I'll dress in a fabulous outfit and set out for a good day. Blaring the songs that made up this season of life and the unexpected making of *The Playbook*. Singing with myself through every green light with my fresh red nails at the wheel. After I parallel park under a flamboyán, I'll pull down the car visor mirror, patting gently the creases of concealer under my eyes. And as I close the visor shut, a smudge of **girl** will be left behind with all the others.

I'll catwalk in my favorite pair of heels and right into the *5th Avenue Coffee Company & 6th Street Diner*, bringing my sunglasses to the top of my head like I'm the main character in every award winning romantic comedy, insistent on **everything good, everything fabulous.**

With my quiche of the day and a café au lait,
I'll open my laptop,
bittersweet,
ready to keep writing.

& on the screen in front of me, it will read...

THE MODERN GIRL'S PLAYBOOK

SAYS EVERY GIRL EVER

VOLUME II

**YES, GIRLFRIEND!
COMING SUMMER 2025**

**WAIT 'TIL YOU HEAR
ALL THE CRAZY NONSENSE
SHE HAS TO SAY.**

scan to order

EPILOGUE

to the girlfriends.
to the girl's girl.
to the girls.

I hope this becomes your new favorite coffee table book. I tried to make it cute so that you'd leave it out all the time and so that it doesn't become just a sideways spine on the shelf. I hope when your girlfriends come over, they love it, too. That you'll laugh together over some of the scenes and talk about your favorite ones. To our content creator girls, please have your way with *The Playbook*. Take these scenes, make them yours, & make us laugh.

In the meantime, if you find yourself faced with a girl moment, whether it's throwing your bra on the ground the minute you walk in the door or chair dancing over the perfect snack or jamming out in your car to just one more song before going inside the house: enjoy it, capture it, share it, and tag me.

@BYMONICAMARIE

& so,
from my wooden barstool
at the big picture window
at my favorite cafe,
I have just applied a fresh coat of red lipstick.
& with my own two hands,
I have rolled the red carpet that is before you,
as you embark back into the modern world.

Strut your stuff
& go on
& get your girl on
in the ways none of us know
how not to.

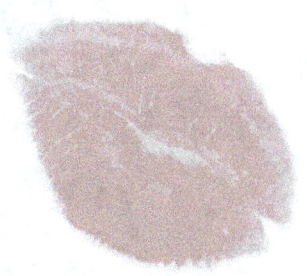

IS SHE WINDOW SHOPPING?
OR CHECKING HERSELF OUT?

& IF SHE'S IN HIGH HEELS
& SHE'S WALKING THAT WALK,
DON'T BOTHER LOOKING HER WAY
BECAUSE YOUR EYES WILL SURELY BURN.

MBALI SCHMIDT

"ALEXA!
PLAY THE
PLAYBOOK
OFFICIAL
SOUNDTRACK
ON SPOTIFY."

YOU GOTTA JUST GO FOR IT.
DON'T THINK ABOUT
WHAT COMES AFTER
OR WHAT CAME BEFORE.
YOU JUST GOTTA
BEND YOUR KNEES,
TAKE A DEEP BREATH,
& JUMP.
JUMP BY ME N Ü

scan to listen

The Playbook [Official Soundtrack]
Playlist by monicamarie_music

MONICA MARIE

Author. Writer.
& dog Mom to the best girl of all time.
HER NAME IS LUNA.
& she is the reason
for 99% of all cancelled plans.

@bymonicamarie
on Instagram

acinomzetrocllc@gmail.com
for inquiries